NATIONAL PARKS

YOSEMITE
NATIONAL PARK

by Maddie Spalding

Content Consultant
Stephen Cunha
Professor of Geography
Humboldt State University

Core Library

An Imprint of Abdo Publishing
abdopublishing.com

abdopublishing.com

Published by Abdo Publishing, a division of ABDO, PO Box 398166, Minneapolis, Minnesota 55439. Copyright © 2017 by Abdo Consulting Group, Inc. International copyrights reserved in all countries. No part of this book may be reproduced in any form without written permission from the publisher. Core Library™ is a trademark and logo of Abdo Publishing.

Printed in the United States of America, North Mankato, Minnesota
092016
012017

Cover Photo: Mikhail Kolesnikov/Shutterstock Images
Interior Photos: Mikhail Kolesnikov/Shutterstock Images, 1; Russ Bishop/Alamy, 4; Red Line Editorial, 7, 25; National Park Service, 9, 42–43; Shutterstock Images, 12, 15, 19, 26, 36, 45; Marc Venema/Shutterstock Images, 17; Yongyut Kumsri/Shutterstock Images, 20; Michael Warwick/Shutterstock Images, 23; Universal History Archive/UIG/Getty Images, 28; G. Seeger/ Shutterstock Images, 34

Editor: Mirella Miller
Series Designer: Ryan Gale

Publisher's Cataloging-in-Publication Data

Names: Spalding, Maddie, author.
Title: Yosemite National Park / by Maddie Spalding.
Description: Minneapolis, MN : Abdo Publishing, 2017. | Series: National parks
   | Includes bibliographical references and index.
Identifiers: LCCN 2016945465 | ISBN 9781680784763 (lib. bdg.) |
   ISBN 9781680798616 (ebook)
Subjects: LCSH: Yosemite National Park--Juvenile literature.
Classification: DDC 917.94/47--dc23
LC record available at http://lccn.loc.gov/2016945465

CONTENTS

CHAPTER ONE

A SEA OF PEAKS

The early-morning sun gleams off a landscape dusted with snow. A skier inhales the crisp air. She drives her ski poles into the powdery snow. The rugged rock formation known as Half Dome towers in the distance. Dark-green pine trees rush past as she picks up speed. Her skis carve out tracks in the fresh snow. A cold wind nips at her cheeks. She leans forward in her skis and plunges down the

Skiing is one of Yosemite's main winter tourist attractions.

Clare Marie Hodges became a Yosemite park ranger in 1918. She was the first female park ranger of the National Park Service (NPS). The NPS was having a hard time finding men to work as park rangers. Many were fighting in World War I (1914–1918). Hodges had been a teacher in the Yosemite Valley School. She knew the park needed rangers, and she knew she was well qualified. She approached Yosemite superintendent Washington B. Lewis with her idea. She expected him to laugh at her. Instead, he agreed. Hodges's example paved the way for future female park rangers.

steep slopes of Yosemite National Park.

Yosemite attracts many visitors in winter. The Yosemite Ski & Snowboard Area offers plenty of opportunities for downhill and cross-country skiing. Millions of people also visit the park throughout the rest of the year. Rock climbers come for the challenge of scaling Yosemite's cliffs. Nature enthusiasts explore the park's groves of giant sequoia trees. Yosemite offers something for everyone.

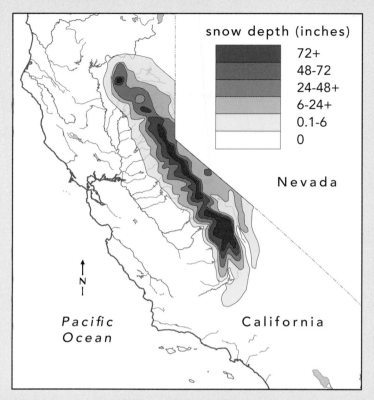

Snow Depth in the Sierra Nevada
The map above shows annual snow depth in the Sierra Nevada. Which parts receive the most snow? How can you tell?

Yosemite is located in California along the Sierra Nevada mountain range. Spanning 748,036 acres (302,719 ha), it is roughly the size of Rhode Island. More than 4 million people visited the park in 2015. This makes Yosemite one of the top ten most-visited US national parks.

The Yosemite Land Grant Act

Early white settlers came to Yosemite Valley in the mid-1800s. Some brought cattle and sheep. These livestock grazed in Yosemite's meadows. They damaged plants. Settlers also cut down trees. They used the trees to build houses.

California senator John Conness wanted to protect Yosemite Valley and the surrounding lands. He wrote a bill. The bill asked the US government to give the lands to California. President Abraham Lincoln signed the bill in 1864. It became the Yosemite Land Grant Act. More than 60 square miles (155 sq km) of land were given to California. This included Yosemite Valley and the Mariposa Grove of Giant Sequoias. Government workers tried to protect this land. But visitors still damaged the resources.

Protecting Yosemite

Environmentalist John Muir visited Yosemite in 1889. He had lived and worked in the area only eight years earlier. But the landscape had changed. Tunnels had

John Muir knew making Yosemite into a national park was the only way to ensure the land was protected.

PERSPECTIVES

Former Park Ranger J. D. Swed

J. D. Swed began his career as a Yosemite park ranger in the early 1970s. He no longer works as a park ranger. But he remembers his first days at the park clearly. He arrived at the park in the night during a rainstorm. He remembers waking up the next morning to the sound of a waterfall. He recalls: "There was snow halfway down the valley floor. It was just spectacular. I had no idea a place like that existed. It was amazing . . . I couldn't get enough of it, and it still affects me that way today."

been carved through giant sequoia trees. Yosemite Valley was littered with tin cans and other garbage. Muir was shocked. He began to fight for the creation of a national park.

Muir wrote articles about Yosemite. He also began writing books about the area. Muir's writings helped convince President Benjamin Harrison to protect Yosemite. Harrison signed a bill on October 1, 1890. This bill created Yosemite National Park.

Conservationist John Muir wrote a book called *The Yosemite* in 1912. In it he described the beauty of Yosemite's landscape:

> *No temple made with hands can compare with Yosemite. Every rock in its walls seems to glow with life. . . . How softly these rocks are adorned, and how fine and reassuring the company they keep: their feet among beautiful groves and meadows, their brows in the sky, a thousand flowers leaning confidingly against their feet . . . while the snow and waterfalls, the winds and avalanches and clouds shine and sing and wreathe about them as the years go by, and myriads of small winged creatures—birds, bees, butterflies—give glad animation and help to make all the air into music.*
>
> Source: John Muir. *The Yosemite. New York City: Century Company, 1912. Print. 8.*

Consider Your Audience

Adapt this passage for a different audience, such as a teacher or a friend. Write a blog post conveying this same information for the new audience. How does your post differ from the original text and why?

CHAPTER TWO

GEOLOGICAL HISTORY

Yosemite National Park is famous for its rugged mountain peaks. These peaks slope down into U-shaped canyons. Miles of lakes and rivers cross through Yosemite's valleys. Waterfalls cascade down cliffs. Natural forces that began millions of years ago formed this dynamic landscape.

Granite dominates Yosemite's landscape.

Mountain Formation

Every year thousands of rock climbers visit Yosemite. They scale the park's steep granite cliffs. More than 95 percent of the Sierra Nevada mountain range is granite.

Granite formation began approximately 100 million years ago. Magma pooled in chambers miles below Earth's surface. This melted rock beneath the surface cooled slowly. As it cooled, it formed mineral crystals. These crystals built up into gray granite rock.

Some magma chambers were underneath volcanoes. A chain of volcanic mountains ran through what is now central California. Magma spilled out onto the earth's surface as lava from these volcanoes. It cooled and formed volcanic rock. Other kinds of rocks also formed under heat and pressure. These were metamorphic rocks. But wind and rain eroded much of this overlying rock. The underlying granite rock was exposed. This happened approximately 65 million

Yosemite's granite cliffs are evidence of the ancient geological processes that formed this landscape.

years ago. Granite is a strong rock. It did not erode as easily as the volcanic and metamorphic rocks.

Earth's crust has fractures called faults. Segments of land called tectonic plates meet at these faults. The San Andreas Fault runs through western North America. Plates along this fault shifted approximately 25 million years ago. Rocks along the fault were lifted upward. These rocks built up and became the Sierra Nevada.

There are no longer volcanoes in Yosemite. But some younger volcanic rocks can still be found along the edges of the park. These are approximately 3 million years old. Other metamorphic rocks such as slate can be found throughout the park.

Glacial Movement

The climate cooled approximately 3 million years ago. Glaciers began to form in the upper Sierra. These large bodies of ice slid down mountainsides. They transported rocks and debris as they moved. Their movement carved out canyons and basins among mountains. Glacial melt and rainwater collected in basins.

Two glaciers remain in the park today. These are the Maclure and Lyell glaciers. They formed between 700 and 150 years ago. The Maclure Glacier rests atop Mount Maclure along the east side of Yosemite. Mount Maclure reaches nearly

Shrinking Glaciers

Yosemite's glaciers begin to melt in the summer. Glacial runoff from the Maclure and Lyell glaciers feeds into Lyell Fork, which branches into the Tuolumne River. This river supplies water to Tuolumne Meadows. Yosemite geologists are uncertain how glacier loss will affect this environment. Some geologists predict that the Maclure and Lyell glaciers may disappear within five years. But they continue to educate the public about the glaciers' importance to Yosemite's landscape.

Melting glaciers formed lakes throughout the park.

13,000 feet (3,962 m). Lyell Glacier is on the slope of nearby Mount Lyell. Mount Lyell is the tallest peak in Yosemite. It rises up to 13,114 feet (4,000 m). Cold temperatures at these high elevations preserved the glaciers. But climate change now threatens them. Pollution caused by human activity releases carbon dioxide into the atmosphere. This has led to a rise in temperatures worldwide. As a result, both glaciers in Yosemite have shrunk by more than 60 percent during the last century.

World-Famous Waterfalls

Many waterfalls cascade from high cliffs in Yosemite. They can be found throughout the park. Large

Geologist Allen Glazner

Allen Glazner is a geologist at Yosemite National Park. He studies rock formations. He says:

One of the things that makes Yosemite such a great place for us as geologists to work is that nature has taken these rocks and polished them for us. We can come out here and literally crawl around on our hands and knees looking at beautifully polished specimens. . . . We can see the relationships among these minerals. We can see into the guts of what was a magma chamber and see what was going on then frozen in time for us.

glaciers carved hanging valleys at high elevations. Hanging valleys are U-shaped valleys high up in the Sierra Nevada. Hanging valleys were shaped by glacier erosion. Streams tumble down these valleys into lakes or rivers below. Many of Yosemite's waterfalls were formed this way.

Yosemite is home to the tallest waterfall in North America. This is Yosemite Falls. It is located in Yosemite Valley near the center of the park. Yosemite Creek feeds into this waterfall.

Yosemite Falls is one of the most photographed waterfalls in North America.

It is 2,425 feet (739 m) above the valley floor. That is nearly twice as tall as the Empire State Building in New York City.

Horsetail Fall is another popular waterfall in Yosemite. It is located in Yosemite Valley. Its cascading water reflects the red-orange glow of sunsets in mid- to late-February. This makes the water look similar to falling lava. Photographers from around the world come to Yosemite to capture this sight.

BIOLOGICAL HISTORY

E levation in Yosemite National Park ranges from
1,800 feet (549 m) to more than 13,000 feet
(3,962 m) above sea level. Many different
habitats exist at these varied elevations. Yosemite's
mountains support a variety of plants and animals.

Vegetation Zones

Yosemite National Park has many vegetation zones.
Vegetation zones are regions classified by climate,

Giant sequoias are the oldest trees in the park and the
third-longest-living tree species in the world.

elevation, and plant type. Climate in the park varies by elevation. Some plants flourish at low elevations. Others only exist at high elevations.

Plants at low elevations in Yosemite belong to the foothill-woodland and lower montane forest zones. The foothill-woodland zone can be found at elevations of 1,800 feet (549 m) on the west side of the park. This area is hot and dry in the summer. It receives little or no snow in the winter. Blue oaks and gray pines thrive here. Plants at elevations of 3,000 feet (914 m) receive more rain. These plants belong to the lower montane forest

Wildflowers bloom in meadows in the upper montane forest zone.

zone. Yosemite's giant sequoia trees can be found in this zone. They grow in three groves along the western edge of the park. Grizzly Giant is the largest giant sequoia in Yosemite. It is located in Mariposa Grove at the south end of the park. This tree is estimated to be 1,800 years old.

Red fir and pine trees grow at elevations of 6,000 feet (1,830 m). They belong to the upper montane forest zone. The Jeffrey pine tree in this zone has bark that smells similar to vanilla. More varieties of hardy pine trees grow at elevations of 8,000 feet (2,438 m). These trees belong to the subalpine forest zone. The climate is much cooler here. As much as nine feet (2.7 m) of snow falls in this area in the winter.

Yosemite's Animals

Yosemite is home to more than 400 species of animals. They range in size from the California ground squirrel to the American black bear. Some of these animals are threatened or endangered. This means their populations have declined.

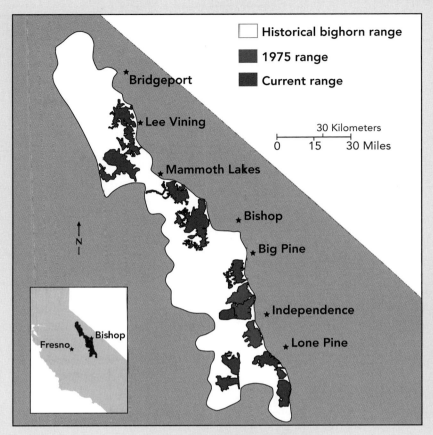

Sierra Nevada Bighorn Sheep Distribution

Biologists released Sierra Nevada bighorn sheep into
Yosemite in 1986. Since then their population has grown
throughout the Sierra Nevada. This map shows how
the population of Sierra Nevada bighorn sheep has
changed over time. How can you tell from this map that
Sierra Nevada bighorn sheep have been reintroduced
into the Sierra Nevada?

Approximately 50 Sierra Nevada bighorn sheep

live in Yosemite. This may not seem like very many.

But there were no bighorn sheep in the park only 100

years ago. Settlers brought domestic sheep into the

A Sierra Nevada red fox was found in Yosemite in 2015.

Sierra Nevada. Domestic sheep carried diseases that spread to wild bighorn sheep. Settlers also hunted many bighorn sheep. The National Park Service (NPS) reintroduced these mammals in Yosemite in 1986. It moved 27 bighorn sheep from surrounding areas into the park. It released 11 more sheep into the park in 1988. But harsh winters in 1994 and 1995 reduced the sheep's population by 60 percent. The NPS released 12 additional sheep into the park in 2015. Biologists continue to monitor and protect this endangered species.

Another animal that disappeared from the park in the early 1900s was the Sierra Nevada red fox.

Trappers hunted these foxes in the 1800s and 1900s. Their fur was used to make clothing. Trapping was finally banned in California in 1974. But it had greatly reduced the red fox population. Today biologists estimate there are only 50 Sierra Nevada red foxes left in North America. Before 2015 the last confirmed sighting of this animal in the park was in 1916. Biologists are not sure yet whether this means that the red fox population is finally rebounding. But they know this animal will be protected in Yosemite.

FURTHER EVIDENCE

Chapter Three introduced you to plant and animal species that live in Yosemite National Park. What was one of the main points of this chapter? What evidence is included to support this point? Read the article at the website below. Does the information on the website support the main point of the chapter? Does it present new evidence?

Yosemite's Wildlife

mycorelibrary.com/yosemite

CHAPTER FOUR

YOSEMITE'S AMERICAN INDIAN HISTORY

The first settlers in the Yosemite area arrived between 8,000 and 10,000 years ago. Archaeologists have found tools such as arrowheads that date back to around this time. These original settlers were the Paleo-Indian people. They were likely the ancestors of the Miwok people who later lived in the area.

Yosemite's rich valleys and abundant wildlife supported people for thousands of years.

The Miwok people lived around the Sierra Nevada mountain range. They included several separate groups. The Southern Sierra Nevada Miwok people lived in present-day Yosemite Valley more than 4,000 years ago. The Central Miwok people occupied what is now the northern part of the park. Approximately 9,000 people lived in the foothills of the Sierra Nevada. The Miwok people called Yosemite Valley "Ahwahnee." This means, "Place Like a Gaping Mouth." Those who lived in this valley called themselves the Ahwahneechee.

The Black Sickness

Spanish soldiers and missionaries arrived on California's coast in the late 1700s. Spanish missionaries tried to convert native people to Catholicism. Spanish soldiers invaded tribal lands. They captured native people and forced them to work as builders or farmers. But some managed to escape. They fled east into the Ahwahnee Valley.

The Spanish carried foreign diseases, which spread to native people. Tribes fleeing east unknowingly carried a foreign disease into Ahwahnee Valley. It spread throughout the Ahwahneechee villages. The Ahwahneechee people called it "the black sickness." Historians believe this might have been smallpox or measles. Whatever the disease was, it proved to be deadly. By 1800 only a few native people remained in the Ahwahnee Valley.

PERSPECTIVES
Cultural Anthropologist Eirik Thorsgard

Eirik Thorsgard works with the NPS and the tribes surrounding Yosemite. He collects information about the park's and the tribes' histories. Thorsgard says:

Even though I'm a park employee, I'm still acting as an advocate for the Tribes. But, I'm also an advocate for the Park Service too. . . . There are some things that if you don't record them, they just get lost. Finding a way to be helpful as that knowledge transfers from generation to generation and finding ways to help these communities record what is important to them is super exciting.

They fled their villages and joined neighboring tribes to survive.

The Ahwahnee Valley remained uninhabited for many years. But the Ahwahneechee leader, Chief Tenaya, convinced his people to return there in 1833. Their population grew. But they soon faced more threats from white settlers.

The California Gold Rush

Gold was discovered in the Sierra foothills north of Yosemite in 1848. White settlers eager to make a fortune rushed to California. They invaded Miwok territory. They set up mining trading posts by the Tuolumne River. They cut down oak trees to make room for these trading posts. Miwok Indians relied on oak trees as a food source. They ate acorns that grew from these trees. Deer were also a major part of the Miwok diet. But white settlers were killing large numbers of deer and other animals. The Miwok people faced starvation.

Miwok Indians began raiding trading posts. They stole clothes and other supplies to survive. They fled into more remote parts of the Sierra Nevada. California governor John McDougall formed a military force to seek out these Indians. This force was called the Mariposa Battalion. Major John Savage led it.

The Mariposa Battalion followed the Miwok Indians into the Sierra Nevada. They came to Ahwahnee Valley in January 1851. This was the first time non–American Indian people had entered the valley. Savage asked Chief Tenaya to sign a treaty. He promised peace if the Miwok and Ahwahneechee Indians

Lafayette Bunnell was a member of the Mariposa Battalion. He began calling the Ahwahnee Valley "Yosemite" in 1851. The name likely comes from the word *uzumati*. *Uzumati* means "grizzly bear" in the Miwok language. The Ahwahneechee were divided into groups called clans. One was called the bear clan. Some historians believe that Bunnell named the valley after this Ahwahneechee bear clan.

Miwok and Ahwahneechee Indians hid from the Mariposa Battalion in Ahwahnee Valley.

would agree to move west into the Fresno River Reservation. But Chief Tenaya refused to sign. His people did not want to leave their homeland.

The Mariposa Battalion responded by attacking the Miwok and Ahwahneechee Indians. But the Indians resisted these attacks. The Mariposa Battalion was disbanded in July 1851. By 1852 a small group of Ahwahneechee Indians remained in the valley. They are the ancestors of many American Indians who live near Yosemite National Park today.

Rock climber and snowboarder Lonnie Kauk is a direct descendant of Chief Tenaya. Kauk thinks about his heritage and his tribe's connection to Yosemite every time he climbs. He says:

> My grandparents raised us to respect and honor where we come from and do good things. When I was a kid my grandma would tell us stories about our people, how they lived, while she weaved her baskets. . . . I'm so honored to be a descendant [of] one of Yosemite's great chiefs. I for sure feel the spirit guiding me through. Many times I stand on top of mountains thinking of my people living in this amazing place. I know the same blood runs through my heart, so when I climb these mountains I [give] all my thanks.
>
> Source: Toyacoyah Brown. "Adrenaline Rush! Meet Native Rock Climber/Snowboarder Lonnie Kauk." PowWows.com. PowWows.com, September 1, 2014. Web. Accessed May 2, 2016.

What's the Big Idea?

Take a close look at this passage. How does Kauk's heritage influence the connection he has with the park? How might his view of the park differ from a non–American Indian's view of the park?

THE PARK TODAY

Visitors to Yosemite National Park can explore all aspects of its history. Tall granite rocks such as Half Dome hint at the area's geological history. Visitors might see mule deer in Yosemite Valley that remind them of the park's biological history. The reconstructed Ahwahneechee village behind Yosemite Museum teaches visitors about early settlers. All of these areas in the park can help visitors

Kayaking is one of the many activities visitors have to choose from during the warm months.

Captain Charles Young

Captain Charles Young was a leader of the Buffalo Soldiers. The Buffalo Soldiers were a troop of African-American soldiers in the US Army. Young was also the first African American put in charge of a national park. He was the acting superintendent of Sequoia and General Grant national parks in 1903. These national parks are located in California, not far from Yosemite National Park. Young and approximately 500 other Buffalo Soldiers worked in Yosemite. They kept poachers and ranchers out of the park. They also built the first trail in the park and built protective fences around trees.

appreciate Yosemite's long and rich history.

Park Attractions

Yosemite is a popular skiing destination in the winter. But there are plenty of activities to do year-round. Visitors who feel adventurous can try rock climbing. The Yosemite Mountaineering School & Guide Service offers rock-climbing lessons for climbers at all skill levels. Hiking is another popular park activity. Hiking trails allow visitors to explore the park.

Glacier Point Road provides access to many popular trails. These trails wind through mountains and valleys. Wildflowers bloom in McGurk Meadow in the summer. Sentinel Dome rises 8,122 feet (2,476 m). Hikers can get a bird's-eye view of the park from this height. Experienced hikers can trek up El Capitan. This trail takes hikers through thick forests. Those who make it to the top can look out on sweeping views of Yosemite Valley and Half Dome.

PERSPECTIVES
Botanist Martin Hutten

Martin Hutten is a botanist for Yosemite National Park. He studies the park's plants. He is involved in the Lichen Inventory Project. This project involves examining lichens to learn about the park's air quality. Lichens are similar to sponges. They absorb material from the environment. Examining them helps scientists find out about air pollution levels in the park. Hutten sometimes climbs trees or rocks to get lichen samples. Hutten especially enjoys this part of his job. He says: "Many jobs have lots of routine. If you're studying elements of nature, I think that routine quickly falls away."

Fire Management

Human influence is constantly changing Yosemite's landscape. Climate change from human activity has led to periodic drought. This has reduced water flow in the park. Animals have lost some of their habitats this way. But not all human influence is bad. Sometimes it is needed to maintain the park's ecosystem.

California has dry and hot summers. Wildfires are common in these conditions. Small fires get bigger as they feed off dry grasses and forests. Wildfires can damage large areas of land. They alter animal habitats. Areas damaged by wildfire may take years to recover. But small fires can benefit the environment. They kill off harmful insects and weeds. They recycle nutrients back into the soil. New plants grow from these nutrients.

American Indians who lived in Yosemite Valley often set small fires. They did this to open up the land and to see predators. Many plants had room to grow after weeds were destroyed. The plant diversity in Yosemite today likely resulted from these controlled fires. Fire managers in Yosemite today also use controlled fires.

Managed fires are one way that park staff preserves Yosemite. Millions of visitors are drawn to this scenic park every year. Protecting the park means millions more will be able to visit in the years to come.

EXPLORE ONLINE

Chapter Five discusses popular activities in Yosemite National Park. The article at the website below goes into more depth on this topic. How is the information from the website the same as the information in Chapter Five? What new information did you learn from the website?

Experience Yosemite
mycorelibrary.com/yosemite

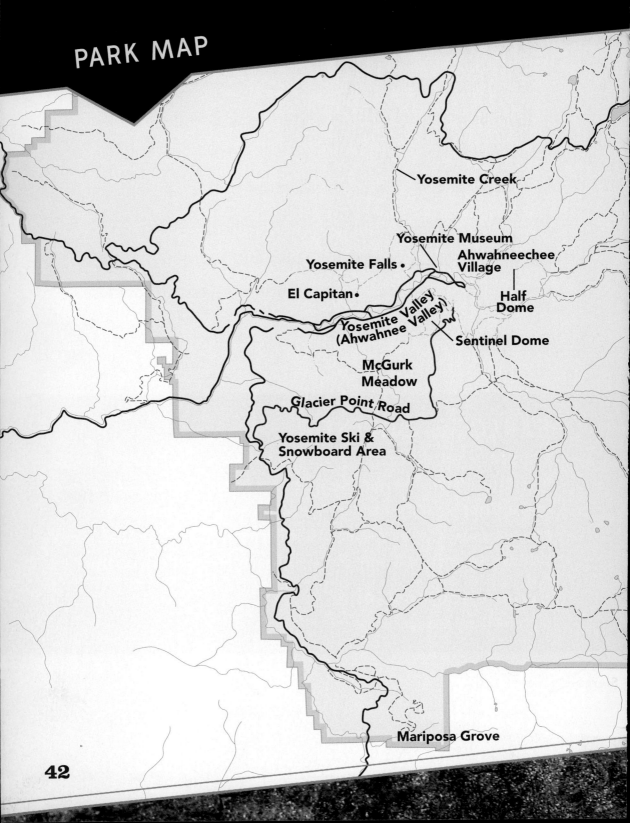

Yosemite Creek

Yosemite Museum

Ahwahneechee Village

Yosemite Falls •

El Capitan •

Half Dome

Yosemite Valley (Ahwahnee Valley)

Sentinel Dome

McGurk Meadow

Glacier Point Road

Yosemite Ski & Snowboard Area

Mariposa Grove

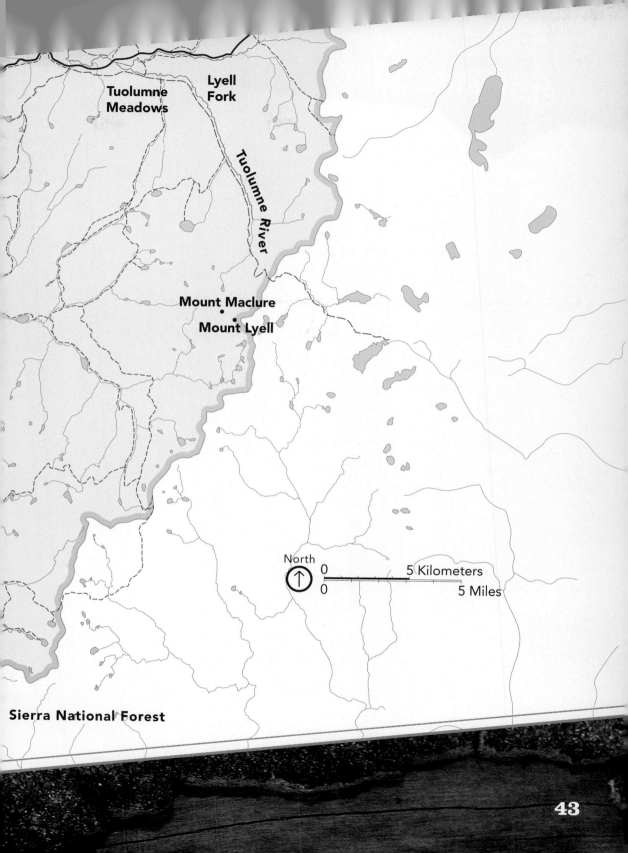

Tuolumne
Meadows

Lyell
Fork

Tuolumne River

Mount Maclure

Mount Lyell

North

0   5 Kilometers
0   5 Miles

Sierra National Forest

STOP AND THINK

Another View

This book discusses the reintroduction of Sierra Nevada bighorn sheep into Yosemite. As you know, every source is different. Ask a librarian or another adult to help you find another source about this subject. Write a short essay comparing and contrasting the new source's point of view with that of this book's author. What is the point of view of each author? How are they similar and why? How are they different and why?

You Are There

This book talks about early settlements in the Yosemite Valley. Imagine you are among the first people to settle there. Write a letter home telling your friends what you have found. What do you notice about the landscape? What plants and animals can you find? Be sure to add plenty of details to your notes.

Dig Deeper

After reading this book, what questions do you still have about Yosemite National Park? With an adult's help, find a few reliable sources that can help you answer your questions. Write a paragraph about what you learned.

Say What?

Studying a national park can mean learning a lot of new vocabulary. Find five words in this book you have never heard of before. Use a dictionary to find out what they mean. Then write the meanings in your own words, and use each word in a new sentence.

GLOSSARY

archaeologist
a person who studies the bones and tools of ancient people to learn about the past

drought
a period of little or no precipitation

ecosystem
a community of animals and plants living together

erode
to wear away

habitat
the place and natural conditions in which a plant or an animal lives

mineral
a substance that is formed under the ground

missionary
a person who is sent to a foreign country to do religious work

poacher
a person who hunts or fishes illegally on someone else's land

reservation
an area of land set aside by the government for a specific purpose

territory
a large area of land

treaty
an official agreement made between two groups

LEARN MORE

Books

Flynn, Sarah Wassner, and Julie Beer. *National Parks Guide USA*. Washington, DC: National Geographic, 2016.

Graf, Mike. *My Yosemite: A Guide for Young Adventurers*. Berkeley, CA: Heyday, 2012.

Mattern, Joanne. *John Muir*. Minneapolis, MN: Abdo, 2014.

Websites

To learn more about National Parks, visit **booklinks.abdopublishing.com**. These links are routinely monitored and updated to provide the most current information available.

Visit **mycorelibrary.com** for free additional tools for teachers and students.

INDEX

ABOUT THE AUTHOR

Maddie Spalding is a writer from Minnesota. She enjoys writing about history and the environment. She has visited a few US national parks and hopes to visit more in the future.